Published by Barbour Publishing, Inc., P.O. Box 719, Uhrichsville, Ohio 44683, www.barbourbooks.com

 Member of the
Evangelical Christian
Publishers Association

Printed in China.
5 4 3 2 1

In Celebration
of the
Savior's Birth

Connie Sue Lora

And the angel said unto her, Fear not, Mary:
for thou hast found favour with God.
And, behold, thou shalt conceive in thy womb,
and bring forth a son, and shalt call his name
JESUS. He shall be great, and shall be called
the Son of the Highest:
and the Lord God shall give unto him
the throne of his father David:
and he shall reign over the house of Jacob for
ever; and of his kingdom there shall be no end.

LUKE 1:30–33

And Joseph also went up from Galilee. . .
unto the city of David, which is called Bethlehem. . . .
And so it was, that, while they were there,
the days were accomplished that she should be
delivered. And she brought forth her firstborn son, and
wrapped him in swaddling clothes,
and laid him in a manger.

LUKE 2:4, 6–7

The shepherds said one to another,
Let us now go even unto Bethlehem,
and see this thing which is come to pass,
which the Lord hath made known unto us.
And when they had seen it,
they made known abroad the saying
which was told them concerning this child.

LUKE 2:15, 17

JAN. 1, 1897

The new year was entered upon with thankfulness, for the unnumbered blessings granted during the old, and was celebrated in our home with our dear children and grandchildren—also brother Lewis and family—the day [was] very pleasant. After the dinner was over presents were exchanged—ours were a nice toilet set from Arvine and Alice, a dozen napkins [of] very nice fine linen from Walter and Sadie and [a] nice hanging lamp from John, all of which we prize for their beauty and usefulness but most of all for the givers' sake.

Then the 138 Psalm was read and we had a blessed season of prayer expressing our gratitude to Him who gave us *all* and implored His blessings still to rest upon us thro this year granting us grace to live for Him, closing with the singing of that beautiful prayer, "God be with you till we meet again."

JOURNAL ENTRY OF TAZETTA CATTELL MALMSBERRY,
GARFIELD, OHIO

Jazetta Cattell Malmsberry, a Quaker minister's wife and my great-great-great-grandmother, penned the previous thoughts in her diary to begin the year of 1897. Her thoughts exemplify for me the meaning of the season—and this book. Friends, family, thankfulness, thoughtful gifts. . .never forgetting the One we look to and why we celebrate Christmas at all.

How do you perceive Christmas? Do you prize Christ's coming to earth as an easy remedy for our sins—or do you prize Him, His love, for the Giver's sake—He who gave His life so that we may live (John 10:10)? This is what the season is really about—not just His birth, but His life. Join with me in exploring past traditions and discover new ways to celebrate as you rejoice in the Savior's birth with the ones you love this Christmas.

We thank Thee, O God, for the return of the wondrous spell of this Christmas season that brings its own sweet joy into our jaded and troubled hearts.

Forbid it, Lord, that we should celebrate without understanding what we celebrate, or, like our counterparts so long ago, fail to see the star or to hear the song of glorious promise.

PETER MARSHALL,
from the prayer "A Christmas Grace"

Hark, hark, the wise eternal word,
   Like a weak infant cries,
In form of servant is the Lord,
   And God in cradle lies.

This wonder struck the world amazed,
   It shook the starry frame;
Squadrons of spirits stood and gazed,
   Then down in troops they came.

Glad shepherds ran to view this sight,
   A choir of angels sings,
And Eastern sages with delight
   Adore this King of kings.

Join them, all hearts that are not stone,
   And all our voices prove,
To celebrate this Holy One,
   The God of peace and love.

THOMAS PESTEL,
from "A Christmas Morning"

Only a Little Town

On all the other nights it had been only a little town, half-hidden in the darkness.

Then came that Night of Nights when Light came to Bethlehem. There was the dazzling glory of the angel choir brightening the skies of the surrounding country. There was the pure white light of the Star that stood over a stable roof. There was the golden radiance emanating from the Baby in the manger, making beautiful the humble stable and everything in it. There was light of happiness in Mary's eyes and the light of love and wonder in the eyes of all who came to behold the little Saviour.

Light travels fast and far. And the Light from Bethlehem still shines brightly today in the hearts of all who love Him.

ESTHER BALDWIN YORK

The wonder of Christmas is that the God who dwelt among us now can dwell within us.

AUTHOR UNKNOWN

According to historical records, the very first Christmas celebration in America occurred in 1607 in Jamestown, Virginia, where forty survivors of the one hundred original settlers tried to boost their discouraged, uncertain spirits by recognizing the birth of Christ in their humble chapel.

Happy Birthday, Jesus

Singing "Happy Birthday" to Jesus is the highlight of our family Christmas celebration. Through the years, having a birthday party for Jesus became a way to teach the children in our family the true meaning of the day, and even though the children are now grown, it remains an established and much loved tradition.

Following a full meal of bowls of steaming soup, warm sandwiches or muffins, and Christmas-colored Jello salad, we enjoy a special dessert—Jesus' birthday cake, complete with one candle. We light the candle, symbolizing that He is the Light of the world, and sing the traditional birthday song to Him. The hostess blows out the candle and everyone feasts on the velvety-soft cake and ice cream. The family then gathers in the living room to hear the Christmas story from Luke, Chapter 2, and all join in singing favorite Christmas carols. Opening our gifts completes the evening of family fun and fellowship.

MARIJANE TROYER

Family traditions are the threads that link one generation to the next.

RICHARD EXLEY

Sometimes I think our Christmas on the frontier was a greater event to us than to any one in the states. We all had to do so much to make it a success. . . .

One universal custom was for all of us to spend all the time we could together. All day long the officers were running in and out of every door [and] the "wish you Merry Christmas" rang out over the parade ground after any man who was crossing to attend to some duty and had not shown up among us. We usually had a sleigh ride and everyone sang and laughed as we sped over the country where there were no neighbors to be disturbed by our gaiety. If it was warm enough there poured out of garrison a cavalcade vehemently talking, gesticulating, laugh[ing] or humming bars of Christmas carols. . . .

The feast of the day over, we adjourned from dinner to play some games of our childhood in order to make the states and our homes seem a little nearer. Later that evening, when the music came up from the band quarters, we all went to the house of the commanding officer to dance.

With a garrison full of perfectly healthful people with a determination to be merry, notwithstanding the isolated life and utterly dreary surroundings, the holidays were made something to look forward to the whole year round.

JOURNAL ENTRY OF ELIZABETH BACON CUSTER,
WIDOW OF GENERAL GEORGE ARMSTRONG CUSTER, UNDATED

From home to home and heart to heart,
from one place to another,
the warmth and joy of Christmas
brings us closer to each other.

EMILY MATTHEWS

Christmas glows in every land,
but hearts just somehow pine
for home and all the loved ones
come joyous Christmastime.

LOISE PINKERTON FRITZ,
from "Home for Christmas"

CHRISTMAS BRINGS JOY TO EVERY HEART

Christmas brings joy to every heart,
Sets old and young rejoicing,
What angels sang once to all on earth,
Oh, hear the children voicing.
Bright is the tree with lights aglow,
Like birds that perch together,
The child that holdeth Christmas dear
Shall keep these joys forever.

Joy comes to all the world today,
To halls and cottage hasting,
Come, sparrow and dove, from roof tree tall,
And share our Christmas feasting.
Dance, little child, on mother's knee,
The lovely day is dawning,
The road to paradise is found
The blessèd Christmas morning.

BERNHARDT S. INGEMANN

Making Christmas Cookies

Making Christmas cookies together as a family is fun and can be a time for growing closer together. Ever since our son Tom was barely more than a toddler, he has helped to make and decorate Christmas cutouts. Most of his adventures in cookie decorating took place at his Amish grandmother's home in the country.

Grandma Saloma would have the cookie dough ready when we arrived so she could help him cut out the different cookie shapes and then bake them. When he was younger, Tom had the most fun eating the prepared cookie dough before any cookies were baked. In keeping with tradition, Grandma Saloma always cautioned him not to eat too much of it so he would avoid a tummyache—and so they would have enough dough to finish the batch. Tom best remembers fingering the gooey dough and thoughtfully contemplating which shapes they would make—making the utmost of decisions.

After the cookies had baked and cooled, Grandma would ice them, and Tom got to add the various sprinkles and colored sugar on top. Of course, the best part was eating the freshly baked cookies with a tall glass of milk and talking with his grandma.

MARIJANE TROYER

Start your own cookie tradition with a loved one this year!

World's Best Sugar Cookies

350°, 10–12 minutes
Makes 7 dozen

Put aside ½ cup sugar and ½ teaspoon cinnamon to mix and use later.

CREAM TOGETHER:

1 cup powdered sugar	1 cup butter
1 cup white sugar	

ADD:

2 eggs beaten with	1 cup Crisco oil
2 teaspoons vanilla	

SIFT TOGETHER AND ADD TO ABOVE MIXTURE:

1 teaspoon salt	1 teaspoon cream of tartar
1 teaspoon baking soda	5 cups flour

Dough may be sticky. CHILL 8 hours or FREEZE 1 hour. Form dough into 3–4 balls to hurry chilling. Once chilled, shape into walnut-sized (½-inch) balls. Roll in ½ cup sugar and ½ teaspoon cinnamon mixture.

Place on ungreased cookie sheet 2 inches apart. Flatten with fork or fancy-bottomed glass. Bake at 350° for 10–12 minutes.

Victorian scrap cookies, popular in the 1800s, were made by securing cutout pictures—scraps— to cookies with a little bit of sugar and water. This was a fun way to brighten the task of holiday cooking, providing a quick and easy way to decorate, as well. These scrap pictures were to be removed from the cookie before it was eaten, as they were inedible. Cookies that were especially meaningful could be hung on the Christmas tree for several years.

Let Christmas be a bright and happy day; but let its brightness

come from the radiance of the star of Bethlehem

and its happiness be found in Christ.

H. G. DEN

The Founding of Bethlehem, Pennsylvania

The city of Bethlehem, Pennsylvania, received its name on Christmas Eve of 1741. The then-settlement congregated in a log cabin that was partially used to house cattle. Later found in a diary was this tale: "Because of the day and in the memory of our dear Savior, we went into the stable in the 10th hour and sang with feeling, so our hearts melted." From that night on, the town was called Bethlehem, in remembrance of when they celebrated the birth of Christ.

Bethlehem is home to many descendents of European immigrants—from Ireland, Germany, Czechoslovakia, Italy, Hungary, and others. It was originally founded by a small group of Moravians, whose influence continues today through many traditions. Moravian cookies, or *ginger thins,* sugar cakes —a yeast bread with potatoes, brown sugar, and butter—and Moravian mints are popular foods throughout the holiday season. Many homes in Bethlehem have miniature nativity scenes, or *putzes,* which can be hand-carved or store-bought. Children gather around the putzes each Christmas morning to hear the story of Christ's birth. Also taking part in the town's celebrations is the Bethlehem Advent Star, which measures 81 feet high and 53 feet wide and overlooks the city and Lehigh Valley below.

Moravian Sugar Cake

Makes 2 cakes, each serving 6 to 8 people

1 small potato,
    peeled and cubed
1 cup water
1 package active dry yeast
⅓ cup granulated sugar
⅓ cup unsalted butter,
    melted
1½ teaspoons salt

½ teaspoon grated nutmeg
3 to 3½ cups all-purpose
    flour
3 tablespoons cold unsalted
    butter, in ½-inch cubes
½ cup dark brown sugar,
    packed
1 teaspoon ground
    cinnamon

In a small saucepan, cook the potato in the water until very soft, about 20 minutes. Cool to lukewarm. Transfer ¼ cup of the potato cooking water to a small bowl, add the yeast, and mix with a fork; set aside.

Mash the potato thoroughly in the remaining cooking liquid until there are no lumps, adding more water if needed to make 1 cup, taking the texture of cooked oatmeal. In a mixer bowl, combine the potato, yeast mixture, sugar, butter, salt, and nutmeg, and mix well. Beat in 1 cup of the flour. Then cover the dough with a tea towel and let rise in a warm place for 45 minutes or until spongy.

Stir down the dough and add enough of the remaining flour to make a soft dough. Turn out onto a floured surface, or use a dough hook, and knead for 4 minutes. Shape the dough into a ball, place in a buttered bowl, and turn once to butter all sides. Cover with a tea towel and let rise for 45 minutes or until doubled.

Punch down the dough and turn out onto a floured surface. Divide the dough in half; cover both portions and let rest for 10 minutes. Cut parchment paper to fit the bottom of two 9- or 10-inch round cake pans and butter the paper. Roll the dough halves out into 9- or 10-inch circles to fit the pans, and transfer them to the pans, patting the dough into place right to the edges of the pans. Cover each cake with a tea towel and let rise 45 minutes or until not quite doubled but puffy.

Preheat the oven to 350°. With your thumb, gently make indentations in the top of the dough, without poking through the dough to the bottom of the pan, at ½-inch intervals. Place a small piece of butter in each hole.

Combine the brown sugar and the cinnamon in a small bowl. Sprinkle over the top of the cakes and bake 20 to 25 minutes or until the cakes are deep golden brown and the butter is bubbling in the center. Let the cakes cool in the pans for 10 minutes before transferring to serving plates. Cut in wedges and serve warm.

Until one feels the spirit of Christmas, there is no Christmas. All else is outward display — so much tinsel and decorations. For it isn't the holly, it isn't the snow. It isn't the tree nor the firelight's glow. It's the warmth that comes to the hearts of men when the Christmas spirit returns again.

AUTHOR UNKNOWN

*S*ome of my best
Christmas memories
are of the simplest
little things. . . .

GWYNETH GAVIN

The ancient custom of the *crèche*—also known as a nativity scene or a *presepio*—is supposed to have originated in Italy with Saint Francis of Assisi. Using live animals and people for the parts of Mary, Joseph, and the shepherds, he conducted a play in a cave near the town of Grecchio about the night of Jesus' birth. A fresh straw-filled manger held a life-sized babe, and through this, the townspeople came to understand the Christmas story. Shortly thereafter they set up their own crèches, and eventually this tradition spread to other monasteries and churches.

Crèches now include figurines made of a variety of materials, including clay, wax, plastic, or wood, to display the people and animals—from the three kings to the lowliest sheep—who participated in the events surrounding the birth of Jesus. These figurines are frequently painted by hand and can be found in marketplaces around the world. Crèches are seen in many homes and churches in the weeks before Christmas. These scenes are meant to look as beautiful and as realistic as possible. Crèches are often found with moss, twigs, or other natural objects, which can extend the display several feet. They also may include figurines dressed in different costumes, transforming a timeless gathering into a modern scene—making us witness to that wondrous event of long ago.

Make Your Own Nativity to Display!

Imagine a barn and decide which elements you want in your nativity. Collect pebbles or larger stones and twigs for the stable walls, roof, and manger, stacking them appropriately. Bind the manger with twine and the stones with plaster of Paris or cement for stability. Build a ladder to the roof or attach a star to the wall. Cut crèche figurines out of plywood or cardboard or mold them out of clay. Be sure to include a way for the figurines to stand vertically. Bring them to life with paint, construction paper, glitter, or other art materials. Figures can include Mary, Joseph, the baby Jesus, and animals in and around the stable. You can even make surrounding scenes of a hill with shepherds, sheep, and angels or a procession of the wise men as they seek the newborn King with their gifts.

In old Europe, it was customary to paint nuts silver or gold and hang them on the Christmas tree. Sometimes a verse or tiny manger scene would be put into a hollowed-out walnut that had been broken in half and hinged so it would open and close.

*May you have
the gladness of Christmas which is hope;
the spirit of Christmas which is peace;
the heart of Christmas which is love.*

AVA V. HENDRICKS

In 1825, JOEL R. POINSETT OF SOUTH CAROLINA, THE FIRST UNITED STATES AMBASSADOR TO MEXICO, CURIOUSLY INQUIRED ABOUT THE BRILLIANT RED "FLOWERS" HE SAW THROUGHOUT THE FOREIGN COUNTRYSIDE. THE LOCAL PEOPLE CALLED THEM "FLAME FLOWERS," "FLOWERS OF THE HOLY NIGHT," OR "FLOWER OF THE NATIVITY," BECAUSE THEY WERE USED IN MEXICAN NATIVITY PROCESSIONS. AFTER OBTAINING CUTTINGS, HE SHIPPED THEM TO HIS RESIDENCE IN SOUTH CAROLINA WHERE THEY WERE CULTIVATED AND EVENTUALLY TOOK THEIR NAME IN RECOGNITION OF DR. POINSETT. POINSETTIAS ARE STILL USED AS DECORATIONS IN AMERICAN AND MEXICAN CHRISTMAS CELEBRATIONS AND CAN RANGE FROM MINIATURE SIZE TO SIX-FOOT TREES.

Celebrations in Mexico start on December 16 for Christmas—the date of the first *posada,* which means *lodgings,* where a couple re-creating the journey to Bethlehem play Mary and Joseph—complete with donkey—seeking shelter. Children accompany the couple, asking for a room at the inn through song as they knock at each door. Replying with a song about having no room, no owners open their houses to the travelers, by tradition, until the last and ninth posada on Christmas Eve. When the procession finally comes to a house or church which bids them to come in, the song becomes one of welcome from the "innkeeper." The children enter and find baby Jesus, sing a lullaby to Him in the manger, and afterwards celebrate with a party and piñatas or a mass.

Christmas with a New Family

The Reverend and Mrs. Giles, along with their children, Jillian and Jordan, have created a distinct Christmas tradition. Each year, they read the Christmas story from a children's book entitled *The Christmas Star* and again as it appears in both the Gospel of Mark and of Luke. After this, the family prays together, and at midnight, with sparkling grape juice in hand, they raise their glasses to toast the birth of the Savior.

This year, the Gileses invited several families in the church to participate. Each family brought with them parts of their own traditions. Some brought cookies, some gifts, but all brought laughter and a sense of belonging. Everyone traveled from house to house, for what is aptly named "The Never-Ending Christmas Party," where the celebration of God's most precious gift is taken to each home for an entire week.

ELISE D. TURNER

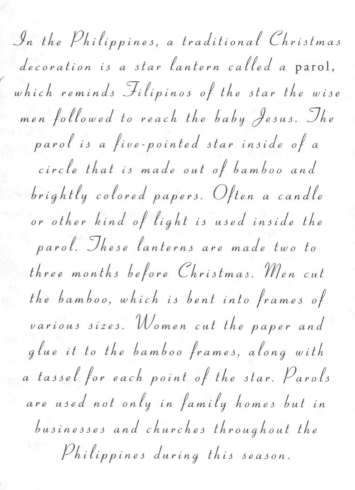

In the Philippines, a traditional Christmas decoration is a star lantern called a **parol**, which reminds Filipinos of the star the wise men followed to reach the baby Jesus. The parol is a five-pointed star inside of a circle that is made out of bamboo and brightly colored papers. Often a candle or other kind of light is used inside the parol. These lanterns are made two to three months before Christmas. Men cut the bamboo, which is bent into frames of various sizes. Women cut the paper and glue it to the bamboo frames, along with a tassel for each point of the star. Parols are used not only in family homes but in businesses and churches throughout the Philippines during this season.

Now when Jesus was born in Bethlehem of Judaea in the days of Herod the king, behold, there came wise men from the east to Jerusalem, saying, Where is he that is born King of the Jews? for we have seen his star in the east, and are come to worship him. . . . And, lo, the star, which they saw in the east, went before them, till it came and stood over where the young child was. When they saw the star, they rejoiced with exceeding great joy. And when they were come into the house, they saw the young child with Mary his mother, and fell down, and worshipped him: and when they had opened their treasures, they presented unto him gifts; gold, and frankincense and myrrh.

MATTHEW 2:1–2, 9–11

*S*omehow,

not only for Christmas,

but all the long year through,

the joy that you give to others

is the joy that comes back to you.

And the more you spend in blessing,

the poor and lonely and sad,

the more of your heart's possessing

returns to you glad.

JOHN GREENLEAF WHITTIER

*M*other's gift to Father was yearly the same but always received by him with surprise and gratitude. She made him slippers of cross-stitched wool which, when completed, she took to our good old cobbler who attached leather soles and heels to the embroidered wool uppers. Mother had obtained the design of crimson roses and green leaves on a black wool background many years before from Godey's Lady's Book *and felt it could not be improved upon. Father often remarked that they gave him perfect comfort and proved it by wearing them in the evening and all relaxed hours.*

FROM THE DIARY OF POLLY MCKEAN BELL,
PORTLAND, OREGON, 1880S

THE LITTLE BRICK HOUSE

$\mathcal{E}$veryone knew Christmastime was near when Edna Malmsberry could be seen scurrying from the corner at the window. Her sewing machine had been positioned there so she could spy the cars pulling up the drive—giving her time to hide the latest surprise. My great-grandmother had gifts for all without fail: Aprons or potholders were usually made for the women, flannel shirts or socks for the men, and one year even held plaid taffeta dresses for six granddaughters. However, it wasn't the gifts that instilled such excitement—it was how they were presented.

Each year, Edna fashioned a large container to hold the wrapped gifts. She called these grab bags, and they were different every Christmas. Best remembered is a "brick"-covered box (most likely arrayed in crepe paper) with the flaps creating the triangle of the "roof." White paper and cotton-trimmed scallops finished the snow-covered roof and eaves. Color-coded strings for age and gender connected to wooden spools of thread and were attached to specific gifts she had made. After the family gathered around the little brick house and each held their spool of thread, Great-grandma gave the word: "Pull!" As strings became tangled and gifts were found, it may have appeared chaotic—but a new grab bag inevitably emerged the following year, and the delightful memories remain to pass to the next generation.

As the Christmas season draws near, we may be tempted once again to "find the perfect gift." We endlessly search the shelves of Wal-Mart or K-Mart for everyone on our lists, and we may even splurge on an expensive gift or two in a specialty shop "just because."

I go to all the trouble and cost because I care and want to make Christmas memorable, but I often end the season feeling both tired and relieved because the Christmas shopping is out of the way. If this sounds familiar to you, try using some of that energy on other gifts this year—meaningful gifts that will bless the receiver. After all, the best and most perfect gift to us was a tiny babe in a simple manger.

He that giveth, let him do it with simplicity. . .with cheerfulness.

ROMANS 12:8

Gifty Ideas

- Bake goodies or do "Gifts in a Jar" for those in your neighborhood with whom you are not yet acquainted. Take along a "Thinking of You" card.
- Energize an "It's been awhile" relationship.
- Spend some time visiting shut-ins. Play a game or take them out for a drive. Many will be lonely and could use a cheery face.
- Participate in coat drives or offer your help to others who have warm–clothing needs.
- Pack a shoebox or two for Operation: Christmas Child to send to children overseas. Share the love of Jesus with them. (See www.samaritanspurse.org/index.asp?section=Operation+Christmas+Child for more information.)
- Make ornaments for fellow church members.
- Assemble care baskets as gifts that go along with a particular interest—one for a coffee or tea lover, or a body care basket with shampoos, lotions, soaps, candles, or bath salts.
- Build a gingerbread house or put "snow" on the windows with young friends.

Remember that it's not about what you spend but the joy you bring to others.

Gifts in a Jar: Ginger Spice Muffin Mix

Requires a wide-mouth quart-sized canning jar, and each layer must be pressed into the jar for the ingredients to fit properly. Ingredients can be layered and the top decorated for a fun look. The recipe can be printed on a label for the front of the jar or done on a hangtag. The jar can also be placed in a large, gathered piece of colored cellophane and tied with ribbon or raffia (remember to attach a gift tag with instructions).

1¾ cups flour
2 tablespoons sugar
3 teaspoons baking powder
½ teaspoon baking soda
1 teaspoon ground cinnamon

½ teaspoon ground nutmeg
¼ teaspoon ground ginger
¼ teaspoon ground cloves
½ teaspoon salt

Combine all the ingredients in a medium bowl. Store the mixture in an airtight container.

ATTACH THIS TO THE JAR:

Ginger Spice Muffins
Makes 1 dozen

1 package Ginger Spice
   Muffin Mix
½ cup butter or margarine, melted

1 egg
1 teaspoon vanilla
1 cup milk

Preheat the oven to 400° and grease 12 muffin tins. In a large bowl, combine the muffin mix with the butter, egg, vanilla, and milk. Stir the mixture until the ingredients are blended. Do not overmix. The batter will be lumpy. Fill muffin tins ⅔ full, and bake for 15 minutes.

Christmas Snow for Window Decorating

Makes enough for 6 small windowpanes

½ cup lukewarm water
½ cup plus about 2 slightly rounded tablespoons mild soap flakes or
  granules
Transparent tape
Assorted doilies or homemade "snowflakes"
Small sponge

In a medium mixing bowl, combine the water and soap flakes or
granules. Stir to dissolve, then whip by hand or with an electric
beater until the mixture looks like stiff meringue and holds its
shape. If making your own snowflake stencils, fold several large
pieces of heavy paper in fourths. Fold in half again to make a
pie-shaped wedge and use sharp scissors to cut out shapes.
Unfold and flatten out before proceeding. Tape paper doilies or
stencils to the inside of the window and use the sponge to dab
the whipped snow over the perforations. Remove the doily or
stencil immediately and allow the design to dry. To remove after
the holidays, just wipe off with window cleaner and a soft cloth.

Christmas Everywhere

Everywhere, everywhere, Christmas tonight!
Christmas in lands of the fir-tree and pine,
Christmas in lands of the palm-tree and vine,
Christmas where snow peaks stand solemn and white,
Christmas where cornfields stand sunny and bright,
Christmas where old men are patient and gray,
Christmas where peace, like a dove in his flight,
    broods o'er brave men in the thick of the fight;
    everywhere, everywhere, Christmas tonight!
For the Christ-child who comes is the Master of all;
    no palace too great, no cottage too small.

PHILLIPS BROOKS

O Lord Jesus, we thank Thee for the joys of this season, for the divine love that was shed abroad among men when Thou didst first come as a little child. . . . May we not think of Thy coming as a distant event that took place once and has never been repeated. . . . May Christmas linger with us, even as Thou art beside us the whole year through.

PETER MARSHALL,
from "A Prayer—For the Day After Christmas"